A Force of
Nature

By

JoAnne Helfert Sullam

DayDreams Studio Press

International Published and distributed by:
Daydreams Studio Press daydreamsstudios@gmail.com

1st edition Publisher's Cataloging-in-Publication data

Names: Sullam, JoAnne Helfert, author.
Title: A Force of Nature / JoAnne Helfert Sullam.
Description: Saugerties
NY: Daydreams Studio Press, 2024.

E book ISBN: 979-8-9863177-2-4
Soft Cover ISBN: 979-8-9863177-3-1

For Londyn

The world gives us infinite opportunities
to create a beautiful life.

Contents

"It's about what you believe.
And I believe in love.
Only love will truly save the world."

—WONDER WOMAN

Introduction

Sitting by my pond drinking a hot cup of afternoon tea, I became amused by three tricolored herons who had just fledged from their nest. The parents had come every year to the pond. But they were shy, and I very rarely saw them or their babies.

At first, the young fledglings jumped from branch to branch in the thick brush over the still water. Then, one by one, they flew to a nearby cedar post that once was the frame to a dock that the pond had long ago reclaimed.

With love and joy in my heart, the young heron's childlike wonder became mine. Remaining a quiet observer of the fledgling herons was enough to resurrect that feeling. I watched as they ventured further and further out from their comfort zone, then finally headed for the sky to fly away to a new life.

As I walked home, the moment and that joy reminded me of a lesson learned a long time ago. It was when I went out in the field as an amateur to study wildlife photography with a professional wildlife photographer who had spent a good amount of time photographing grizzly bears and eagles in Alaska. But when he was back in New York he would invite me to go out and photograph local and migrating birds. On that particular day we were looking for the great American egret, who had migrated to New York for the summer and was spotted nearby.

It was late afternoon when we found the beautiful white heron with the sun-colored beak and long black legs. He was hunting in the marsh only a few yards away. The sky was just turning pink and golden as it readied for the night. It reflected in the water the marsh grass and ever so slightly in the white feathers of the bird.

I held up my camera to my eye to take a photograph.

My friend gently touched my arm and said, "No. The light isn't that good anymore." He turned to look at me and whispered, "Just enjoy the moment."

So we stood there in silence, our eyes immersed in the spectacular, peaceful experience of nature in its purest form. It was in this shift of focus from trying to capture an image on my camera to surrendering to the moment that an unexpected feeling came over me. It was a well of gratitude that bubbled up from a place beyond my time on this Earth. It was a force of nature that lived in me but had often been silenced by the chatter in my brain and the sleepwalking busyness of my days with an endless to-do list. But in that moment, my spirit awakened for the beauty, the abundance, the diversity, and the simple pleasure of the joy of living and being one with nature. I needed nothing from it. It needed nothing from me; we were just both able to be.

A true gift and valuable lesson about living in the moment and on how to be a true force—one with nature.

To become a force of nature one must be able to feel the full force of love, happiness, and joy. We must dig deep into our hearts and take a journey of self-discovery. Leave our comfort zones and venture out to find one's true place and purpose in life and with nature.

It takes self-awareness of one's thoughts and movements. It takes practice to live in the now.

And you will know when it has happened. It's on the days that you can't wait to get out of bed and when you can't stop smiling.

After thirty-five years and counting of serving and observing nature and its wild creatures, one of the biggest lessons I've learned is to be present in the endless moment of now.

A journey that I wrote about in my memoir *Evolution of a Wild Heart.*

The practice of living in the moment can give perspective on the past and help build a better future.

I believe that we can all become a force of nature for the betterment of ourselves in reconnecting with Mother Nature.

In this book, I will share some of my observations and lessons for nature that my wild friends have taught me. My hope for anyone who picks up this book is that they will discover that living in harmony with the earth and nature, instead of on the Earth, using it up without giving something back to our unique planet. Together we can bring great joy and appreciation for life. We can all become a force of nature for the good of all.

Because only love can save us and the abundant, beautiful world that we share.

"Choose only one master—Nature."

–Rembrandt

Our Greatest Teacher

"Choose only one master—Nature."

—REMBRANDT

Nature has always been our greatest teacher. From birth to the grave, we've learned everything from our Mother Earth.

Humans have studied nature under a microscope. We produce substances, materials, and mechanisms in order to synthesize similar things artificially that mimic nature...

It's called biogenetics.

A simple example is the hummingbird and helicopter.

We learned how to make planes and to fly by watching birds.

Spider's silk studies led to inventions such as bulletproof vests, tires, and surgical sutures.

Through trial and error, we learned to build houses, make fire, and ride horses to create transportation with man-made machines.

Faster and faster we go. But where are we really going?

Has technology come with a price? As more and more animals go extinct, and water and air become more polluted, depression is at an all-time high. Humanity has become dependent on pharmaceuticals, recreational drugs, alcohol, cigarettes, and many other addictions to help us feel good. Health issues have become an epidemic as cancer and disease take over so many.

Exercise and wholesome, organic food are no longer part of our everyday life. And come at a high price.

Our future is in our children's hands, yet they spend most of their time with some form of electronics and looking at screens indoors.

How many of us in our busy daily lives stop to take time to watch a sunset? Explore the outside world with a childlike wonder?

Could it be possible that the noise of modern life and electronic distractions, along with the pursuit of material things, have drowned out our inner voice and natural instincts? While our true selves cry out to feel connected to something bigger than ourselves?

So how does one return to the wisdom of the earth and become a force of and for nature? How can we learn to be kind and have better self-awareness and create social responsibility? How do we work with nature as our ancestors did when collecting herbs for healing and listen to the language of Mother Earth as she warns us of upcoming challenges, as well as gifting us with her amazing natural abundance?

To breathe deep, slow, purposeful breath of pure joy is such a gift. So is the breath of gratitude. A breath of love. The breath of life for the Earth and all its endless wonders and mysteries.

Here is a small test to find out where you're at in self-awareness and a small way to receive the wisdom of Earth's amazing creations…

(Tip) Keep a small notebook
or journal with you to use with this book.

Or go (https://joannesullam.com/pages/a-force-of-nature-bonus)

to download a free exercise book with fun, nature-inspired bonuses.

The first step to becoming a force of nature:

Take one minute of your precious time with a pen and pad to bring forth a new awareness… Be spontaneous and without judgment; simply observe your own feelings.

Practice:

Be still, and listen to the silence within and around you. Become aware of the chatter going on in your head.

It's okay if you don't feel anything or feel much; don't judge, just be.

Take a deep, slow breath, then exhale, becoming aware of your surroundings. Now take a moment to center and release, then write down three words to describe what you see or experience and, most importantly, feel.

You can do this as many times as you need to or would like. In your home, in the yard, a garden, at work, by the sea, or sitting under a tree. Anywhere where nature is or where you can visualize. See and feel the nuances.

You can even do this exercise with the people in your life. As you observe you will discover what lifts your spirit and what drains you.

Examples of places where you can do this short exercise: At Home, outside your home, at work, with technology favorite places in nature, with your pets

Nature is our teacher, healer, mother. What can you learn, discover, or be inspired by? Make a list in your workbook or journal.

Comfortably Numb

Hello? Is there anybody in there?
Just nod if you can hear me.
Is there anyone home? Come on now
I hear you're feeling down
Well I can ease your pain
Get you on your feet again
Relax
I'll need some information first
Just the basic facts
Can you show me where it hurts?

–"COMFORTABLY NUMB," *THE WALL*, 1979, PINK FLOYD

Have you become comfortably numb?

If you had to measure yourself in percentages…

100%: Totally numb to your life and the world around you. Such as when you wake in the morning and go through the day, and as you go to bed at night you're unsure of what you ate for dinner or even if you ate at all. Then passing into oblivion, and when you awake you have no recollection of your dreams prior to beginning your new day.

10%: Life is blissful and joyful, feeling happy and excited, like an innocent child who lives for each moment, filling one's day with magic and wonder. When that child lays their head down to sleep, they recall the day's experiences, feeling both exhausted and fulfilled. Reliving the best moments before sleep brings dreams of more wonder heading into the next day. Expecting joy and discovery and ready to tackle another adventure, anticipating one's dreams will come true.

Though life is never going to be perfect, stress and pain will always show up, as sure as the sun sets and rises. Yet there is beauty to be discovered in what some may conceive as imperfection. As that is part of becoming and growing.

What percentage are you at? Where do you honestly put yourself? There is no right or wrong, just awareness.

How nature does it…

"That's death and life, you see. We all shine on. You just have to release your hearts, alert your senses, and pay attention. A leaf, a star, a song, a laugh. Notice the little things, because somebody is reaching out to you. Qualcuno ti ama. Somebody loves you."

—Ben Sherwood

Amplify the Senses

"That's death and life, you see. We all shine on.
You just have to release your hearts, alert your senses, and pay attention.
A leaf, a star, a song, a laugh. Notice the little things,
because somebody is reaching out to you.
Qualcuno ti ama. Somebody loves you."

—BEN SHERWOOD

The basic senses of the body are sight, hearing, smell, taste, and touch; each helps us gather information, as well as form an image of our world. These are key to making decisions in the moment and can trigger what is retained in memory.

Animals in the wild use these five senses to aid in the most important aspects of survival—escaping danger, finding food, and selecting mates. And they must keep their senses as keen as possible since their survival often depends upon it.

Humans are similar, such as an artist. A painter who uses colors, a sculptor who uses touch, or a musician who uses sound, for example. They have one thing in common—they train themselves to enhance a particular sense, depending on their artistic discipline, or even train themselves to use all of their senses at the same time.

In modern life we may become complacent and distracted, possibly not even noticing if one or all of our senses have been dulled; however, if we dig deeper into each of these senses, we can train ourselves to gather information about sounds, textures, sights, tastes, and smells. Experiencing a heightened sense of joy within our physical being to become a true force of nature.

So, let's take a dive in to each one…

Sight and Vision

"Sight is a function of the eyes, but vision is a function of the heart. The bravest sight in the world is to see a great man struggling against adversity. If my ship sails from sight, it doesn't mean my journey ends, it simply means the river bends. In time of difficulties, we must not lose sight of our achievements."

–Lucius Annaeus Seneca

Sight

Eagles are said to have the best vision of all animals. They have binocular, panoramic vision and a heightened sense of color vision and can see UV light. They can see a small mouse from up to three miles away. Eagles can see colors more vividly than humans. An eagle's eyes are almost as big as a human's.

Eagles have evolved to fit their survival needs, habitat, or environment. All which have a lot to do with their evolutionary changes.

Good eyes for one animal may not be so good for another.

Humans have evolved to have three types of cones in the retina that allow us to recognize the colors blue, green, and red. This has been part of our evolutionary needs; however, an artist has a visual awareness that can take their eyes to places most are unaware since they respond to light. Colors are chameleons of the light and are a big part of what a painter studies. In nature, light is always changing from moment to moment. The artist's eyes study this movement since their eyes are always moving around the canvas of life, taking in as much as they can.

Conversely, with the invention of computers, we are unnaturally staring at a fixed screen for hours. This is called "computer-vision syndrome." Therefore, short-sightedness is becoming a growing problem, and more people now have eye strain.

Will our eyes evolve and adapt over time? And, if so, will it improve the quality of human life on Earth?

What's interesting are painters who are legally blind, yet they still paint and create. How can this be?

They have become a force of nature and go beyond what is visibly in front of them by training themselves to use their power of second sight.

Again, the eagle comes to mind, as they are incredible birds, flying the highest of all. In many ancient cultures the eagle is said to be the closest messenger to the heavens/universe.

Which brings me to second sight, an extrasensory perception when a person has a "vision" about future events before they happen, called ***precognition***: the psychic phenomenon of seeing or becoming aware of events in the future.

We do this every day in the simplest of ways. Visualize going to get a cup coffee or tea and voila! You're there sipping away.

How amazing that a bird can see so far in the distance and fly so high. And a blind person can create a work of art full of depth and color. It seems that there is more to sight than meets the eye.

We *can* all be very selective about what we focus on. A simple example is when you buy a car you begin to notice the same car everywhere.

We can train the eyes to be stronger with eye exercises. But more so, we can train our eyes to be like the artist and the eagle.

How can one begin to become a force of nature and grasp the power of the eagle's sight and an artist's vision?

Practice:

Wherever you are, look around, and focus on anything blue…

How many things did you count that were blue?

Now close your eyes…and without looking, how many things do you remember that were red?

Practice:

Choose a scene in nature, and as you focus, pick out anything green. Then close your eyes again, and think of the color green.

After you open your eyes, focus only on this color.

Do this with yellow, then with blue.

In the beginning, stick to basic colors. The idea is to just create more of a sense of awareness with your vision.

Look for patterns and shapes that you can break down to geometrics.

This goes for patterns in your life and works with second sight.

Practice:

Second sight.

Looking within to see the future. Observe yourself as you are now.

Without judgment, observe yourself with a different perspective, as someone else would see you.

Look for patterns and habits that you developed that maybe you've been unaware of.

At the beginning of the day, visualize how or who you want to be that day.

At the end of the day, go over in your mind's eye anything that you saw in yourself that you might want to change.

Now try visualizing your next big goal. Begin with small steps…

First, see yourself where you want to be. Every day, visualize one step you can take toward that goal as an eagle or an athlete or an artist would.

But always remember, there is joy in the journey.

An athlete visualizes getting the ball to go where they want and winning the game. An eagle who can see a mouse three miles away doesn't think twice about what it does. After a lot of practice, the eagle does it with grace and ease.

An artist sees the painting in their mind's eye before they even lay down the first stroke of their paintbrush filled with color.

If you have poor or little eyesight, consider the artists that are legally blind and still paint a beautiful picture.

Most of the time, we're visualizing past events and putting them in our future.

Practice living in the *now*.

And remember to look in the mirror.

You are beautiful, inside and out. You are a force of nature with the eyes and spirit of the eagle and the foresight and talents of an artist. Paint your own beautiful future.

***The eagle is an amazing totem animal,
and you can read more about using this energy in the back of the book.*

***Or, for an inspirational and relaxing video,
got to my YouTube channel for seven characteristics
of the eagle as a spirit guide @
https://youtu.be/O-xRG261GrM?si=BEqOaztgL8dVZ9ZA***

Sound/Hearing

"A bird does not sing because it has an answer.
It sings because it has a song."

–Chinese Proverb

Sound/Hearing

Hearing is the first sense that we have when we're born and the last to go when we pass.

We're also born with an innate fear of loud noises (and falling).

If hearing is the first sense we have and the last one we lose, it can be assumed that it's evolutionary and important to our survival.

As with almost all our senses, we've become overstimulated by noise.

Traffic, TV, barking dogs, sirens, and endless chatter around us and in our heads have an effect on our mood and focus.

Human hearing is affected by both pitch and volume.

Sound and vibration may help assess danger, like the smoke alarm or a siren. And can also soothe us with whispers of comfort via a simple hum or a song.

It was nature's way for different senses to become more prominent as each species adapted to their evolving environment.

While a human may be able to hear a sound from about a hundred yards away, your pet dog can hear up to five hundred yards away. An elephant's amazing hearing allows it to communicate over long distances and hear sounds up to one hundred and fifty miles away.

Sound has as much to do with vibrations as it does with what one hears.

Cymatics is the study of visible sound. The vibration of sound shows us the transformational nature of sound and matter. The practice of cymatics goes back at least a thousand years to African tribes who sprinkled grains on the taut skin of drums to predict the future.

Leonardo da Vinci noticed that vibrating a wooden table on which dust lay created various shapes.

Water is one of the strongest conductors of sound, providing a visual representation of a sound in much the same way a snowflake under a microscope displays its intricate beauty.

The human body is made up of roughly 60 percent to 75 percent water!

Sound guides us and shapes us, yet is an intangible force, as we cannot see what it's doing to our own bodies.

The scientific study done by Japanese scientist Masaru Emoto proved that words matter, as he was able to influence rice with love, hate, and indifference. The rice that he spoke words of encouragement to fermented and flourished. The rice that he spoke to with hate turned black. And the one he showed indifference to rotted.

Even though it's invisible to others, our own internal dialogue (the voice in your head) can be the loudest and have the most influence on what we speak.

It's usually the most negative.

Hearing is a passive activity.

Positive hearing activity: Listening to a song you love, a bird singing, laughter, and any loving words.

Negative hearing activity: The cruel voice in your head, too many load noises, and other berating of ourselves.

Listening is an active activity and in my opinion is an art form. One that takes practice and a level of skill to achieve.

Silence is said to be golden. Yet it's so hard to come by. When not available, we can shut down and become easily distracted when we need to focus.

What are we hearing and what are we listening to? How does this all affect us as humans in the world of endless noise and negative overstimulation? And what can we do about it?

Become a force of nature like the elephant, who feels the vibrations of sound to find water, love, and create family bonds.

Practice hearing:

Be silent. This gives the brain a break and gives one a chance to refocus.

You could go outside take a deep breath and listen to the sounds around you.

Try to focus, even for a moment, on any sounds of nature.

If you can't go outside, you can still do this at home.

Listen to the sounds around you, then separate them and focus on one at a time. See how each one makes you feel.

Work on eliminating, one at a time, the sounds that cause unrest.

Practice listening:

When conversing with someone, take in the words they're saying without judgment, interrupting, or waiting to talk.

Repeat the last thing they said for clarity. This can help one be a better listener and is helpful to others and yourself. It can help clarify one's inner voice and slow down the world of chaotic sounds that don't benefit us.

Practice humming:

Do this for a few minutes every day. It helps to reset and relax the body, mind, and spirit.

We can all feel the good vibrations by making room to listen to the inner joy and songs of our being.

"Smell is a potent wizard that transports you across thousands of miles and all the years you have lived."

–Helen Keller

Smell

Besides elephants, bears have an incredible sense of smell, even better than a hound dog. A bear's sense of smell is three hundred times stronger than a human's.

Human sense of smell may not be our strongest sense, compared to animals, but it is remarkably accurate. The strong relationship between smell and memory is due to the brain's anatomy. Smells go straight to the emotional control center, the limbic system, where memories and emotions are regulated by the amygdala and hippocampus. Smell is also closely related to taste, as you might have discovered when you had a cold or been stuffed up.

So how does one awaken a sense of smell?

Practice:

Reawaken your brain's processing of scents by paying attention to neglected smells, such as the smells of nature, like pine trees, flowers, and fresh fruit.

Essential oils can stimulate our senses and create powerful effects on our mood. Different scents, like peppermint and eucalyptus, can invigorate the mind, while lavender and jasmine have calming properties. Even the scent of citrus fruits, like lemon and orange, can refresh the senses. Take note of different scents that bring up memories or emotions, and create new memories around them.

Taking short, shallow breaths can boost your sense of smell more than taking one deep sniff. This technique is similar to how dogs and cats explore a new scent and can improve your nose's ability to detect smells.

Exercise: Regular exercise has been found to improve one's sense of smell.

Take a walk outside with the propose of collecting smells, and note how they make you feel.

Write down what you've discovered. Take the top three smells that help improve your mood—one for energy, one for rebalancing, and one that evokes a beautiful memory.

"One cannot think well, love well, sleep well, if one has not dined well."

–Virginia Woolf

Taste

When you see a rabbit munching on those alfalfa greens, it's hard to believe that rabbits have twice as many taste buds as humans.

Like humans, both rabbits and dogs can distinguish between salty, bitter, sweet, and even sour.

Dogs and cats have taste buds that detects the flavor of water. This helps them crave water when needed for hydration, especially after consuming salty or sugary foods.

Water's taste is influenced by its mineral composition. For example, high levels of sodium chloride result in a salty flavor, while high levels of magnesium can create a sweet or bitter taste.

Rabbits never eat hot food. Conversely, us humans like our coffee and food hot.

Yet hot drinks and food can affect and dull your taste sensitivity. So, if you're someone who enjoys hot drinks with meals, it's important to keep in mind that this can lead to a decline in taste sensitivity.

So how can one improve their sense of taste like a rabbit and still enjoy a hot meal?

Practice:

1. Transform mealtime into a sensory experience. Elevate your dining experience by savoring each bite. Treat mealtime like a game. Can you *name that spice?*

2. See and taste food as a healing, nurturing art form by paying close attention to visual presentation. Take in every flavor, texture, and spice that you consume.

3. As we age, our taste buds begin to dull; however, we can still stimulate our taste buds with moisture. Moisture is essential to spread food throughout the mouth to coat our taste buds. Fresh lemon juice is known to increase saliva flow and impact how foods taste.

4. Explore new foods. Step out of your comfort zone or spice up your dishes. To add some excitement and variety to your dining experience, be adventurous, and try new, unfamiliar dishes.

5. Document your culinary adventures by starting a food diary. Jot down any new foods and spices you want to try or have already tasted. Describe the experience in detail, such as the flavors, textures, and aromas. Note any recipes or cooking methods used with the new ingredients.

We humans can also improve our taste buds. With minimal effort, we can become a force of nature and savor our food as much as a rabbit who loves their hay and grassy fields.

Bon appétit!

"In rivers, the water that you touch is the last of what has passed and the first of that which comes; so, with present time."

—Leonardo da Vinci

Touch

Evolution has given manatees poor vision, good hearing, and incredibly sensitive facial whiskers that allow them to explore different textures in high resolution, a process called "active touch." Active touch, in simple terms, is just touching. Like the sensation of running fingers over an object. It differentiates from passive touch, where stimulation is from external object movements. The tactile sense acts as both receptors and tools for physical exploration.

Many consider manatees to be magical creatures due to the numerous mysteries and legends surrounding them. Centuries ago, sailors even mistook manatees for mermaids—human-like beings believed to dwell in the oceans.

A manatee's flipper bones resemble a human hand, and like a human hand it aids in movement, feeding, and object manipulation. They even have nails at the end of each flipper. Manatees also possess such a refined tactile sense that it enables them to "feel" objects in the water from a relatively far distance. A manatee's body hairs detect water displacement of less than a micron. To put that in perspective, one human skin cell is twenty to forty microns across! In addition, objects measuring forty to fifty microns are the smallest things that can be seen by the unaided human eye.

A manatee's entire face is about as sensitive as a person's fingertip, and the fingertips are the most sensitive part of a human body.

This was the manatee's evolutionary solution to murky waters and perhaps lead to human curiosity and mass love for this sea creature.

Artists, such as sculptors and musicians, who play instruments have enhanced their sense of touch. Also, using our cell phones has heightened this sense of touch in our fingers. Yet many are not self-aware of this sense. We wash and scrub our bodies and face, then slap on lotions, while becoming desensitized to touch. As incredibly, humans have become germophobic, forgetting that the one thing that made us feel the full force of love is each other's touch.

So how does one become a force of nature with a magic touch?

Practice:

1. Awareness. As with the other senses, being consciously aware of what you're doing is important, like a sculptor touching different materials. And using adjectives to describe how one feels physically and emotionally. For example, identifying by touch if something is soft, rough, cold, or warm. Then writing a word or two identifying the object, then describing if it was a positive or negative experience and why.

2. Besides your fingertips, the palms of your hand are very sensitive as well. Practice palm-touching when out in nature. Place your open hand on the trunk of a tree and close your eyes for a moment as you inhale a deep, slow breath. Then, without judgment, allow yourself to feel the texture and the emotions that come up.

   Do this same exercise at the beach; pick up a handful of sand, and let it run slowly through your fingers. Do this also with water from a stream, ocean, or even your faucet.

3. Ask first, and if someone agrees, give them a hug or touch their shoulder or their hand. As you do so, send them love and good-will, and note how that makes you feel. (Most do this openly with their pets but can sometimes feel vulnerable with people.)

Get in touch with your feelings as to why you might feel this way or if you dislike "space invaders."

What experience did you have that made you feel this way?

Write down what you would like to work on to improve your human connections.

Practice can make us become a force of nature with one enchanted touch.

"One touch of nature makes the whole world kin."

—WILLIAM SHAKESPEARE

"The only real valuable thing is intuition."

–ALBERT EINSTEIN

The Sixth Sense: Intuition

The dictionary definition of the sixth sense is "a power of perception like, but not one of, the five senses: a keen intuitive power."

The philosopher Aristotle was a pioneer in attributing humans with the five traditional senses: sight, hearing, touch, taste, and smell; however, if he were to classify animal senses in modern times, the list would be more extensive. Many animals have extrasensory capabilities that enable them to perceive the world in extraordinary ways beyond human comprehension.

Also, some studies have revealed a clear connection between emotional states and the strength of the electromagnetic fields produced by our hearts and brains. It shows that negative emotions can diminish the field while positive emotions can strengthen it. This reveals that we can connect on many different levels.

Echolocation is the word which enables dolphins, whales, and porpoises to locate prey in environments with limited or no visibility in the depths of the oceans where they live.

Due to the fact that sound travels more effectively in water than air, it makes sense that dolphins have evolved to rely on this three-dimensional visual picture of their surroundings, created solely through sound waves, similar to a sonar device. The sound waves that bounce back to them allow the dolphin to pinpoint objects and aid in navigation, hunting, obstacle avoidance, and social connections.

Dolphins also possess advanced cognitive skills, such as recognition, memory, reasoning, communication, and problem-solving. Their complex limbic system emphasizes emotional depth.

Dolphins exhibit high cognitive abilities with a neocortex containing more neurons than humans, chimpanzees, and elephants, despite differences in brain size and structure.

Dolphins have always had a strong connection with humans, enabling them to perceive dangerous situations and amazingly have shown a readiness to help humans and other animals in need.

Their psychic abilities (or sixth sense) seem to be enhanced.

The bottlenose dolphin has an exceptional *seventh sense*—the ability to detect electricity.

It makes you wonder how our human invention has affected nature and these highly sensitive animals, as well as our own biology.

As far as the sixth sense goes, owls holds a special place. The symbolic meanings of the owl represent intuition, hidden knowledge, and transformation across different cultures. To be graced with their presence often implies increased awareness and imminent, significant transformations.

An owl not only symbolizes intuition but the embodiments of wisdom. It's their exceptional sensory abilities to navigate in darkness, combined with their unique physical traits, like the silence of their wings, that have enhanced their cultural significance and links them to wisdom.

Owls also possess exceptional observation abilities.

Revisiting the artist and creatives who have developed this owl-like talent of exceptional observation skills, artists are known to possess the ability to tap into unseen, powerful energies that can occasionally take over, causing the creator to enter a time warp and disappear into their work.

Something that nature also must possess, though remains scientifically undiscovered. Still, we are living in exciting times when the veil is being lifted on the intelligence of nature and our deeper connections to the Earth, the universe, and all living things. Some of us need this proof, though others born more "sensitive" to this knowledge, or have enhanced their own being, already know this in their hearts to be true.

Speaking from my own experience, part of this progress is from first observing, then sharing the story in an art form, guiding the viewer/listeners along a path that one sets the stage for. Yet, in this process, there must be a letting go of the control that the computer or one's mind often demands to enable thoughts to give way to feelings and an inner knowing. This process is not defined in words as much as it feels *right*. In turn, we then know what doesn't feel right. Remaining in that truth determines what needs or wants to be.

It is, in a way, a form of trusting and faith, which logic and the thinking brain has nothing to do with. Rather, releasing control of the mind to allow connection to the heart and its wisdom.

It's like the dolphin feeling the electricity and the owl having the confidence to fly in the dark.

This is the power of and the force of nature using the sixth sense of intuition. It combines all that we have learned and the practices of enhancing the senses. It allows us to tap into the most powerful sense of all.

So how can one learn when we have been taught otherwise or have been overstimulated by the outside world?

Small steps and practice...

Practice:

1. **Practice stillness of the working mind.**

   Like the owl observation, be aware of thoughts and feelings at the same time.

   Do they match up?

2. **Keeping the body relaxed and the mind active.**

   Did you ever notice that when in the shower or bath or on a walk your mind suddenly comes up with the answer to a problem you've been wrestling with? This is nature working from within.

3. **Watching and being one with nature.**

   Do nothing in nature but allow your mind to wander. This will not only calm the body, but it also allows your mind to guide you without your control, leading you to answers- you're seeking to pursue your best life—one of joy.

4. **Trust your heart it knows what is doing.**

   Yet mistakes are inevitable. When this happens, give it another try. We learn by repetition. At the very least, it's an opportunity to learn something about yourself.

Your time on Earth is sacred. Become a force of nature and swim with dolphins. Feel the life within you, fly with the wise owl of faith into the darkness of the unknown to become the finest version of yourself.

The Elements

One can use the powers of the elements to become a force of nature.

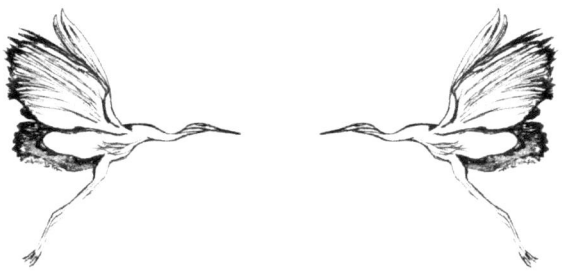

Air

The air element can be compared to the intellectual powerhouse among the elements, representing innovative ideas, clear thoughts, and eloquence. It symbolizes sharp mental abilities, new possibilities, and a refreshing sense of optimism. Like a rejuvenating breeze, it adds energy, vigor, and a hint of magic to the mix.

Breathe deep and take in life.

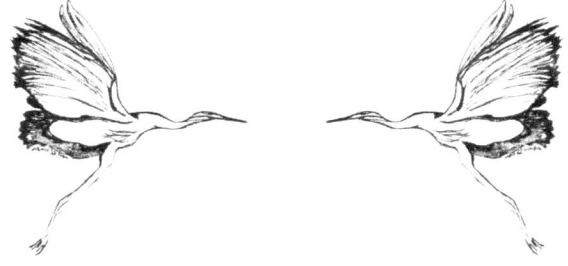

Fire

The element of fire personifies the strength of one's passion, creativity, and inspiration. It represents the capacity to transform ideas into reality.

Harness the energy of life to ignite your passions.

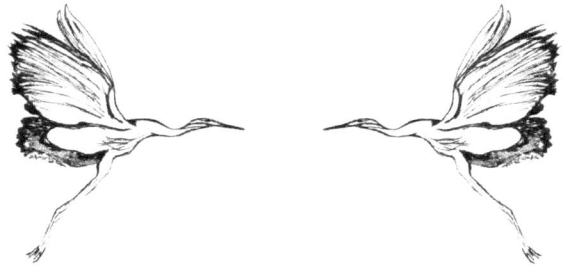

Earth

Earth embodies stability, existence, endurance, and grounding, serving as the cornerstone of all solid elements. It personifies life and is associated with empathy. Earth's traits include reflection, thoughtfulness, and self-examination.

Connect with nature by letting your bare feet touch the Earth directly for energy.

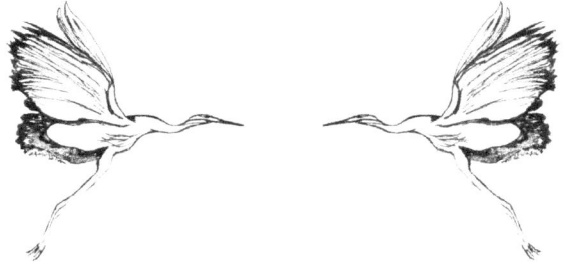

Water

Water symbolizes purity and wisdom, vital for the body's function, reflecting its properties to enhance well-being and revitalizing the body, soul, and spirit.

The power and memory of water is a reflection of one's emotions.

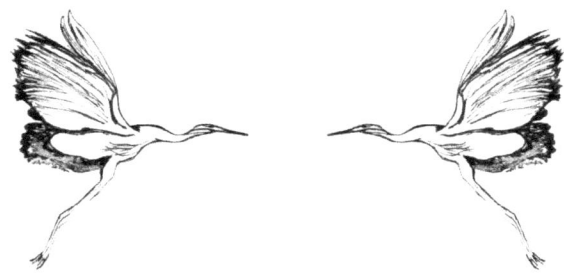

Space

Space acts as the container for all the remaining elements. It encompasses the dimensions of height, depth, and width where everything exists and moves.

It serves as a gentle reminder that we are complete and interconnected with everything around us. Move through it with purpose and care.

"Your time is limited, so don't waste it living someone else's life. Don't be trapped by dogma, which is living with the results of other people's thinking. Don't let the noise of others' opinions drown out your own inner voice. And most important, have the courage to follow your heart and intuition."

–STEVE JOBS

Create a Mistake

"Take chances, make mistakes. That's how you grow."

–MARY TYLER MOORE

The Pottery Wheel and Superglue

Is a mistake always a mistake, or is it an opportunity for something new?

A scientist accidentally invented a reusable, low-tack adhesive while trying to create a strong adhesive. Voila, the Post-it was invented.

The wheel was first used in pottery in Mesopotamia, then in chariots. The wheelbarrow emerged in ancient Greece and was later adopted in China. Wheels were originally used for activities like pottery and milling in ancient times before evolving for transportation in chariots. It took hundreds of years of trial and error before we drove the first car.

Babies are master artists at falling, and it's said they fall around seventeen times per hour while learning to walk, but it doesn't hinder their progress. Falling is an integral part of the learning process, just like taking those first magic steps. Each misstep is an opportunity to get to a better place and to arrive at the goal of discovering something new.

We have gotten so used to instant gratification and are so hard on ourselves and others for failing. Yet falling and failing are part of the process of learning and creative discovery.

So fail up fearlessly to your own discoveries, and walk through life like the force of nature you are.

"Do not fear mistakes. You will know failure. Continue to reach out."

—BENJAMIN FRANKLIN

Wash Away Fear
and Tame the Worry

The fear reaction is a powerful physical response activated by an impending danger, while anxiety is the sensation of worry or unease regarding possible future occurrences.

How does nature deal with fear?

Wild animals release their trauma by moving on as quickly as possible.

Biophobia, fear or aversion to nature, is increasing in society, especially among children, due to excessive technology use. It's natural evolutional fear of snakes and spiders, for example, that has gotten out of control.

Fear is a fact of life and can be a lifesaver. All creatures have it. We call it our fight-or-flight response.

Has it taken over our lives by means of the media, family, etc? Has a trauma, or something else that's unnamed in our body, taken over our minds? Is it irrational, creeping up at night or in the early morning when we least expect it?

Knowledge and Transformations is found by becoming the observer of self and nature and marrying the two.

Practice:

Washing the fear away. When showering, imagine as you clean yourself that you're washing your fears away.

Reminder: The deer that gets chased by the lion and survives gets back to living as quickly as it can run and be free from the threat. It's not to say that we should ignore our pains. Nature wants us to be free of them versus the cage of suppression.

Tame the Worry

Worrying hinders our ability to focus on the present and our future potential. Worry can rob one of peace of mind and leaves the mind and body exhausted. It can impact our environment and personal development. It diminishes the effectiveness of modeling progressive behavior. It takes our mind away from the importance of focusing on key tasks necessary to achieve them. It removes the power of synergy, as when everything falls into place. Worry steals the value of our emotional connections and the significance we attach to them. Time is a precious commodity, and wasting it on worrying about things we cannot change is unproductive.

Practice:

1. Focus on impressing yourself, rather than others.

2. Avoid creating unnecessary problems by projecting everything that can go wrong.

3. Surround yourself with supportive individuals, and remove those who steal your life force.

4. Address problems, not with worry but with productive, creative problem-solving.

5. Propose to yourself: What if (fill in the blank) does work out?

Here are some essential needs that can be addressed and improved with a focused mind.

- The need for basic necessities, like food and shelter
- The need to keep moving, letting emotions flow like a river or a slow-moving lake, to avoid stagnation
- The need to feel important and connected
- The need for growth and evolution in every aspect of life
- The need to give back, as giving to others and to life is a valuable gift to oneself

Learn to be your best friend, and ask yourself: What would you advise your best friend to do?

Learn to Be Creative at Problem-Solving

"Success is not final; failure is not fatal.
It is the courage to continue that counts."

–WINSTON CHURCHILL

Nature is always healing herself
and is amazing at problem-solving

Study those who you admire and their ways of problem-solving.
Then ask yourself, What haven't I tried before?
It's like looking at a painting upside-down.
It allows you to see things from a new perspective.

Get back to the core of your being

Nature and animals are true to their being; in other words, they are who they are. We're all born to be who we truly are. When you were a young child, you clearly had likes and dislikes. You were born with a unique personality, and there will never be another you.

In nature, animals are born with distinctive traits; however, changes in their behavior are shaped by their environment, family, and tribe or community.

Like the deer or a bird, a herd of elephants or a pride of lions, if one is grounded in nature, then they can retain most of their original persona and contribute to society. Like the hundredth monkey who washed his food.

As humans, we have been overly influenced by our surroundings. If we have been abused or experienced extreme trauma, we can lose our true selves and walk through life with undefined longings. That longing, I believe, is our true self calling to us.

So, how does one discover who they really are?

Practice:

Go out for a walk in nature as the child you once were.

Remember the things that got you excited. What were they? What did you spend your free time thinking about and doing when you were four or five years old?

At the same time, take in the air and sights and sounds of nature. They will help you remember.

When you get home, write the top three things you remembered. Which one will you bring into your life from now on?

"If you find yourself in a situation where you are not inclined to make a change but feel pressured or influenced by others, let other opinions pass through your spirit like a breeze through the leaves of a tree."

–JoAnne Helfert Sullam

Synchronicity

L et your instincts and the synchronicity of the flow of life guide you. Life is ever-changing, and like the butterfly we must change and migrate to a new, palatable environment throughout the seasons of life.

Decision-making isn't always easy. It's said that the average person makes thousands of decisions every day. Approximately two thousand every waking hour and one decision every two seconds! Some decisions need to be made on the spot. Like an antelope being chased by a cheetah, one cannot waste a moment with indecision. More than likely, as a human you'll recognize the urgency. Yet one can get on the hamster wheel of life rushing through everything, unsure of where they're going. On the flip side, we can procrastinate and drag things on longer than necessary.

Decisions, change, and growth come in waves. It can be as frightening as an ocean riptide that you didn't know was there or as serene as floating down a slow-moving river that you thought was a still pond. Small choices can take you to a place you didn't plan to go.

Yet listening to the silence beforehand can give a gentle cleansing of thoughts before taking action.

In the shadow of trying to create balance with life, we believe it to always be attainable. Yet it can seem elusive.

Perhaps being off-balance is the path to growth and becoming in balance? Look for synchronicity to guide you.

Create New Habits

What makes you sing? For me, it's being with nature. It gives me stealth, strength, and reminds me that I'm alive.

It takes away the drone of everyday habits with its predictability toward nature's unpredictability.

At home I'm safe but at times unable or unaware that I'm not growing or learning something new.

If we're not growing, we're fading.

What habits benefit you, and which ones do not?

"The biggest difference between money and time is that you always know how much money you have, but you never know how much time you have…"

−UNKNOWN

Time Versus Money

We once traded in spices and tulips.

Nature's commodities are fresh air, organic food, clean water, and to play and work with an intent to not waste life or time.

Consider: Anyone can make and sometimes lose money. But no one can ever get back their time.

"You will continue to suffer if you have an emotional reaction to everything that is said to you. True power is sitting back and observing everything with logic. If words control you, that means everyone can control you. Breathe, and allow things to pass."

–BRUCE LEE

Say What You Mean, and Mean What You Say

Nature and wild creatures do what they say they will do with action. They speak with their actions and give us the truth of their being and intentions. So often, we speak and make promises to ourselves and others that we cannot or do not keep; the truth of our intent is also uncertain.

To become a force of nature, one must strive to be kind truth tellers.

Yet controlling one's emotions sometimes is like trying to control the waters of an overflowing river during a storm. If we never tried to, it can feel impossible.

When reflecting on a blowup we had with someone, we may regret what we said or did. Consequently, what can one do? At times, we need to take action; other times, we need to use our words. So, in what way, could one learn to control what they say and their emotional state?

**Remember words have meaning far beyond the surface of what you are saying.

(Think of your words as the water you drink and who you say them to as the rice.)

When is it right for someone to let it out or to reflect before reacting? It can take practice to learn to control emotions, and it can start with words and action.

Practice with small things, like annoyances. Analyze what the trigger is and the annoyance and why. This gives one the skill and one small step to work toward first before going on to the bigger ones.

Factors to always take into account:

You can never tame a hungry lion, pet a sick cat, or hug a bear that has been woken from its den.

So, rule out hunger, fatigue, and any underling sickness. They can be physical, mental or spiritual. Identifying what the cause is can help immensely. When one is comfortable with knowing the cause and can put the small things in check, one can work on the bigger triggers.

This isn't to be like a robot, as every living creature has emotions. But to learn to not have them run amok every day. To find a peaceful place for a productive flow of thought and purpose of wants, needs, and to say what you mean and mean what you say and do.

Be a Force of Nature—BABE

Balanced: Strive for balance in life, even during times of imbalance, as they may signify periods of growth leading to self-transformation. Recall the buffalo that faces a storm and the cow that flees. The wise buffalo understands that facing challenges leads to desired destinations, rather than avoiding persistent shadows.

Abundant: Abundance is always found within one's heart. It appears like the rising sun when we are grateful for what we already have.

Being: Be a beautiful being who is able to live in the moment, enhancing one's day with the joy of just being alive.

Enlighten: Enlightenment comes with each day when openness to learning, loving, and change is enabled.

"None of us, including me, ever do great things. But we can all do small things, with great love, and together we can do something wonderful."

—MOTHER TERESA

The Power of Love

In the heart lies the epicenter of our existence, where the magic of body, mind, and soul intertwine.

Ultimately, we are emotional creatures, and I'm convinced that our emotions lead both our minds and bodies. Love, being the most potent emotion, has the ability to conquer fear, anger, and instill hope within and unite all living things.

Rectification of a Life Worth Living
Inspire Yourself

Journal for ten minutes, and make seven leaps to reach one dream goal

1. With an attuited of gratitude, write three things you're grateful for.

2. Choose one goal, and write for ten minutes creating seven steps you can do now to get there.

3. Repeat every seven days until you get where you want to go. But remember, it's the journey that maters the most. Repetition is important for each intention as we alter our dreams, change, and evolve.

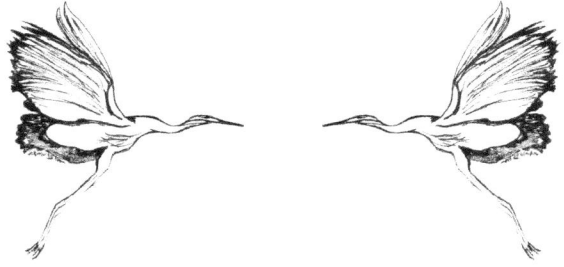

Dream Big and Start Small

A bird builds its nest one stick at a time.

"Picture yourself in that situation using your imagination first, and don't worry about the steps to reach it, as the ideas will naturally come to you."

–JoAnne Helfert Sullam

"He who has a why to live can bear almost any how."

–Friedrich Nietzsche.

Finding you *why* will motivate you when things are hard and keep you focused and feeling alive.

In my memoir, *Evolution of a Wild Heart*, I wrote about wildlife that I've cared for who inspired me. One in particular was a small bird who gave me hope during a dark period in my life. Whenever life becomes difficult, as it surely happens at times, I still remember that bird's brave heart and am inspired to carry on.

"Sailing the Seven Seas of Your Why"

There is much mythology associated with the number seven, since it appears repeatedly throughout history and in stories and has its own place in culture, history, and religion.

A rainbow has seven colors, there are seven Wonders of the Ancient World, seven days of the week, seven dwarves in *Snow White*, seven days in the creation story, seven chakras, and so on.

"Sailing the seven seas" is an idiom referring to sailing all oceans and creates a romantic view of exploring the seas of our planet. Sailing the seven seas has been mentioned in songs and books.

Spiritually, the number seven is associated with insightfulness, truth, wisdom, knowledge, and self-analysis.

For whatever reason, the number seven holds a strong palace in the significance of the human experience.

It's also interesting that there have been so many books written on the topics of self-awareness and finding one's deeper reason of *why*. Yet we rarely dig deep into the *why* of what we do; however, just know it can be enlightening and sometimes emotional when you get to the seven layers of your reason for doing what you're doing but can be worth the journey, as it will help keep you be honest with yourself and the truth, the bottom line of your dreams. A method to help you stop wasting your precious time, which will not serve you in the end.

If you explore, you will find a deeper meaning of why you do the things you do in your life. Because the first few answers we give are usually superficial. Digging deeper will unveil your true *why* and acts as the catalyst for achievement or in some cases abandonment of an idea that has a weak foundation. Because a lack of clarity on your *why* can lead to feelings of overwhelm, anxiety, and unfulfillment.

For the worksheet to explore

"Sailing the Seven Seas of Your Why"

Go to (https://joannesullam.com/
pages/a-force-of-nature-bonus)

Adopting a Spirit Animal

The qualities of a "spirit" or a "totem animal" can be used in a range of circumstances and has been in many cultures, dating back centuries as well as in today's modern world, and the teachings still remain relevant.

Some examples—stock trading is described to be a bear or a bull market. Or we refer to a person as having the spirit of a lion or to be as clever as a fox, and so on.

When one needs a little help with confidence, energy, self-care/love, courage, hope, balance, abundance, or enlightenment, animals can be a great source of inspiration. As well as for times when one may need a leg up on a situation that life has thrown their way. Having a spirit animal is a great way to adopt a needed characteristic in life for one's self-development and resourcefulness in business and/or relationships.

Here are a few general characteristics of selective animals, some of which are mentioned in this book with adoptable traits associated with a particular animal for many common human needs. It's important to note that each of us has our own perception and feelings related to nature and wildlife. So be open to new experiences, and use your own intuition about what is needed.

Spirit animals in alphabetical order:

1. Bear

The bear spirit animal stands for courage, inner strength, and self-reflection. It teaches us to face our fears and find a balance between rest and action. Bears remind us of the importance of solitude in healing and personal growth.

2. Butterfly

The butterfly represents transformation, joy, and the courage to embrace changes leading to personal growth. It symbolizes the ability to go through life's challenges with grace and emerge stronger. The butterfly encourages us to appreciate beauty, adapt to new beginnings, and find joy in our journey.

3. Cheetah

The cheetah reflects high energy, focus, and the ability to pursue goals with determination. It represents speed and agility. Cheetahs encourage quick thinking and swiftly acting on opportunities.

4. Deer

The deer symbolizes nobility, grace, and sensitivity. It is respected across various cultures, representing regeneration, respect, and a balance between strength and kindness. The deer encourages us to be vigilant and to tread lightly through life.

5. Dolphin

The dolphin spirit animal embodies joy, harmony, and inner strength. It teaches us about the importance of community, cooperation, and protecting those in need. Dolphins remind us to approach life with a sense of playfulness and to cherish freedom and kindness in our interactions. Dolphins encourage balance and communication.

6. Eagle

The eagle is seen as a symbol of enlightenment and rebirth, guiding those it chooses toward achieving greater heights and understanding. It encourages embracing challenges with courage and determination, much like a warrior preparing for battle. This majestic bird also signifies the importance of viewing situations from a higher perspective.

7. Elephant

The elephant is associated with remarkable emotional strength, deep wisdom, and a calm stability. It teaches us the importance of resilience, the value of community bonds, and the power of gentle leadership. Elephants encourage us to embrace patience and honor our relationships with kindness and respect.

8. Fox

The fox spirit animal is linked with qualities such as cleverness, adaptability, and resourcefulness. It is recognized for its ability to navigate complex situations with ease and for its keen observation skills. The fox also symbolizes the importance of acting swiftly in decision-making, encouraging flexibility, and the ability to quickly adjust to new circumstances.

9. Giraffe

Giraffes encourage us to look at life from a higher perspective and embrace foresight. They stand for grace, peace, and individuality, urging us to stretch our abilities and pursue what seems out of reach. Their calm and gentle approach to life reminds us to maintain patience and kindness in our interactions.

10. Gorilla

The gorilla spirit animal represents strength, compassion, and leadership. They emphasize the importance of family and community and guide individuals toward nurturing their relationships and leading with kindness and wisdom. Gorillas also symbolize the strength to face challenges with patience and to act with integrity.

11. Hawk

Hawks symbolize clarity, confidence, intuition, power, and wisdom. They are seen as messengers, guiding individuals to trust themselves and embrace change. Hawks encourage a clear vision for the future and represent successful attainment, suggesting abundance and self-reliance.

12. Koala

The koala conveys a strong connection to the Earth, symbolizing tranquility, peace, and protection. It embodies calmness, encouraging appreciation of the present moment.

13. Lion

The lion is known for its bravery, confidence, and assertiveness. It represents strength and the courage to face life's challenges. As a symbol of leadership and personal power, the lion encourages us to tackle obstacles with nobility and grace. Lions encourage asserting oneself and taking control while emphasizing the importance of community.

14. Manatee

The manatee emphasizes the importance of embracing our feelings. It advocates self-expression and emotional release to facilitate personal growth, symbolizing trust and advising us to believe in our instincts and the natural flow of life.

15. Owl

The owl spirit animal is deeply connected to wisdom, mystery, and intuition. It inspires us to see beyond the surface and unmask deception. It represents an ability to navigate through darkness, both literally and metaphorically, offering clarity and insight into unseen truths.

16. Panda

The panda represents peace, patience, and a positive attitude. It encourages one to embrace a gentle power and maintain a good sense of humor. The panda also represents the importance of taking care of personal space and keeping balance in life.

17. Rabbit

The rabbit spirit animal is associated with quick reflexes, fertility, and abundance, symbolizing the ability to move swiftly through life's challenges. It represents creativity, vigilance, and the importance of listening to your intuition.

18. Red Panda

The red panda teaches the value of gentleness, patience, and the strength found in solitude. It guides toward happiness independently while emphasizing the importance of close social relationships. This unique animal represents originality and nonconformity, encouraging balance, kindness, and the peaceful path in life.

19. Raven

The raven symbolizes harnessing the power of your intellect. Using magic, the raven encourages transformations and dream realization. It is a guiding force though struggles and represents healing with inner strength.

20. Rhinoceros

The rhinoceros stands for strength, protection, and solitude, embodying robustness and the power to overcome obstacles. It carries a message of confidence and self-assurance while urging individuals to trust in their own power and to approach life's challenges with determination.

21. Shark

22. The shark is linked with intelligence, power, mystery, and innovation. It embodies determination, speed, and a fighting spirit, teaching us the importance of action and directness. Sharks encourage us to go after what we want with efficiency and not to be deterred by challenges.

23. Tiger

The tiger spirit animal symbolizes courage, power, and independence. It encourages bravery, self-confidence, and trusting your instincts. Tigers inspire us to face challenges with strength and grace. Tigers encourage confidence and the fulfillment of one's duties.

24. Turtle

The turtle teaches wisdom, patience, and the importance of a steady pace. It symbolizes longevity, protection, and a deep connection to the Earth. Turtles remind us to take life one step at a time and to protect ourselves and those we care about.

25. Whale

The whale symbolizes deep emotional healing and inner truth. It encourages us to dive deep into our emotions to discover the wisdom and peace that lie beneath the surface. Whales are seen as record keepers and carriers of ancient knowledge.

26. Wolf

The wolf represents family, intelligence, freedom, and instinct. It symbolizes the importance of trusting one's intuition and the value of both independence and community. Wolves guide us to follow our instincts and find our way with a pathfinder or teacher.

If you're interested in a spirit animal that you don't see below, refer to my website's email list at https://joannesullam.com or subscribe to my YouTube channel at https://www.youtube.com/channel/UCc57pZVm-RojsZUHFH_bTfA for more inspirational videos.

About the Author

JoAnne is an advocate for conservation and has worked with wild and domestic animals for most of her life. A fine artist, producer who writes, lectures and films animals. Donating her time and art for conservation, JoAnne has been featured in The New York Times, Who's Who in America, Art Business News, and Polo Players Magazines. She is the author of a number of books including Evolution of a Wild Heart. She has worked in film and television with celebrities and animal/ environmental advocates. She has spoken at special events including Kent State University, The Salmagundi Art Club, Yellowstone Park, as well as numerous schools and nature centers. JoAnne is a licensed wildlife rehabilitator, animal handler and consultant who lives in the Hudson Valley with her dog Foxy and many wild and domestics critters who stop, stay, rest   for as long as they need too.

You Are A True Force Of Nature!

If you found this book usefull or inspirational in anyway.

Please consider giving a copy as a gift to someone you care about.

It is available in print and digital.

Consider writing a review on amazon, goodreads, or the platform of your choosing.

It would be greatly appreciated.

Your feedback is incredibly valuable for helping independent authors like us to reach a wider audience.

For bulk book orders email us at: daydreamsstudios@gmail.com

For a downloadable cool freebie and additional resources, go to: https://joannesullam.com/pages/a-force-of-nature-bonus

Or to book joanne helfert sullam to speak at your event
Please visit: https://joannesullam.com/pages/speaking-1

Or email us at daydreamsstudios@gmail.com

For upcoming retreats/ workshops go to:
https://joannesullam.com/collections/workshops

Thank You!

www.ingramcontent.com/pod-product-compliance
Lightning Source LLC
Chambersburg PA
CBHW051326120626
46547CB00015B/2415